PARALLELS

Parallels

Published by The Conrad Press Ltd. in the United Kingdom 2021

Tel: +44(0)1227 472 874
www.theconradpress.com
info@theconradpress.com

ISBN 978-1-914913-32-7

Copyright © René Dee and Chris Yates, 2021

The moral rights of René Dee and Chris Yates to be identified as authors of this work have been asserted in accordance with the Copyright, Designs and Patents Act 1988.

All rights reserved.

Printed and bound in Great Britain by Clays Ltd, Elcograf S.p.A.

Typesetting and Cover Design by The Book Typesetters.
www.thebooktypesetters.com

The Conrad Press logo was designed by Maria Priestley.

PARALLELS

Selected Poems of
René Dee and Chris Yates

Chris (left) and René, Rugby, August 1968

'The poems of my Friend would, in a great measure, have the same tendency as my own and that though there would be found a difference, there would be no discordance in the colours of our style.'

William Wordsworth of Samuel Taylor Coleridge, preface to Lyrical Ballads, 1798

René
To those who inspired me to write.

Chris
To my mother Madeleine who taught me to read.

Contents

INTRODUCTION
Why this book? — 13
About René — 13
About Chris — 14
Acknowledgements — 15

FEAR
Suddenly — 19
Waiting for Terror — 19
Conversations in the Wilderness — 21
Why Can't They See? — 21
Nightmare in Narnia? — 22
All Words Mean Something — 23
Five Minutes to Ten — 24
Whose Business? — 25

TIME
The Run — 29
Now Boys Again — 30
Going Nowhere Fast — 31
Paging Miss Chia — 32
Jogging a Kowloon Promenade — 33
Two Late — 34

WAR
With God on Our Side — 37
21st Century Paradox — 39
Brambles in the Hedgerows — 39
Wellington's Injunction — 40

FOOTPRINTS
Followers of the Fox's Path — 45
And Did Those Feet…? — 46
The Big Walk — 47
Messages from Under Foot — 48
Snow Simile — 49
Natter — 49
South Downs Way — 50

ROOTS
Sepia — 53
Roots — 54
Graffiti Bandits! — 56
This England — 56
73 Whitepit Lane — 57
Parallax — 58
Loving Old Wisdens — 60

TREADMILLS
Train Opus — 63
Scrap Heap Blues — 64
Courage at the End of the Conference — 65
Waiting for Roy — 66
The Train — 67

LOVE

The Initiation	71
Unspoken	73
Summit	74
Decibel Love	75
Here Today, Gone Tomorrow	76
Cold Flame	77
Twenty-first Birthday	78
Hot Gums	80
Lunch	80
Apple Tree Bay to Berowra	81
Castello di Uzzano	82
A Melbourne Park	83

DEATH

Tempus Fugit	87
Picking up His Baton	88
A Frail Eternity	89
From Weimar, with Love	90
Samaritans' Nightshift	92

MATES

Friendship	95
The Rakes' Progress	95
Emotional Pasta	96
Meeting at Boat Quay	97
Misfits Redux	99
An Afternoon's Drinking	100

TRAVEL

In the Deserts of this Earth	105
Rainforest Man	106
The Voyage	107
The Lonely Guillemot of Dún na nGall	109
Not so Much a Street, More a Way of Life	110
Fig Andalus	111
Indonesian Evening	113
Singapore Working Girl	114
Distant Return	115
Flight Fragment	115

MEDLEY

Shopping for God	119
Vaginal Vortex	120
Canapés to the Death	121
Patriot Game	122
Cross	123
Berlin	124

Introduction

Why this book?

In 1965, both regular soldiers in the Intelligence Corps, René and Chris met in a chilly army billet, then sustained their friendship over fifty-six years, which amazingly included thirty-five years in which Chris lived in Australia and René lived in the UK. They like nothing better than to get out of class into the playground of real-ale pubs and agree on family and friendship; then disagree on almost everything else. Seemingly alike, there are regular bouts of opposite views expressed that bind them even more. One day in 2009 – of course in a pub – they decided to collaborate on this book.

About René

René was born in Switzerland but has lived in the UK since 1949. After an inauspicious schooling he joined the Intelligence Corps as a boy soldier at the age of sixteen and went on to gain Marine Commando status, attached to a Marine Commando Brigade in Singapore. In 1966 he left the army and travelled overland to Nepal and back from London for three months. The next twenty years saw him lead and organise specialist adventure travel expeditions through North Africa and many other parts of the world for his own, and several other, specialist adventure travel companies. This experience, especially in marketing and promotion, led him to become co-director of the Daily Mail Ski Show and then seventeen years with the Royal Horticultural Society rising to become managing director of its Horticultural Halls and Conference Centre. During this period, he formed a still-operating, marketing collective of primary venues: The Westminster Collection. At the same time, he became interested in poetry and an active member of several poetry societies involved in competitions and recitals. In 2003, he organised and staged his own recital during the Brighton Festival Fringe entitled *The Poetry of War and Conflict*. This was repeated in September that year at the Sussex Arts Club, also in Brighton. His book, *Sweet Peas, Suffragettes and Showmen: Events that Changed the World in the RHS Halls* was published by Phillimore in 2011.

About Chris

Born in 1944 on the Isle of Wight, Chris grew up in the British Army, moving from barracks to barracks in three countries, attending eight schools. He joined the Intelligence Corps at eighteen, escaping often unhappy military life after only three years. Corporate life in organisational development in Australia and the Asia Pacific region petered out with early retirement in 1999. That was followed by university teaching, management consulting and copy-editing. Along the way, he got hold of a bachelor's and master's degree in English, an OU diploma in creative writing, and a petered-out PhD thesis. In retired life he co-

compiled the military souvenir booklet, *An Intelligence Corps Miscellany* and is working on an anthology of poetry. He is the editor of The Rose and The Laurel, the annual journal of the Intelligence Corps, and of *Sub Rosa*, published three times a year by the Friends of the Intelligence Corps Museum. Written in his fifties and sixties, many of his poems touch on tensions of national identity, work and people; friendship is a constant, sometimes undeserved. Chris lives in Bedfordshire.

Acknowledgements

Thanks to Adrienne Dalton who provided the title *Parallels*, and to Glenys Palmer for her proofreading.

Fear

Suddenly

Suddenly, life is there; crinkled and crying,
red, puce and gasping for air,
each time, a miracle to share.
Suddenly, the reason for living; laid bare.

Suddenly, life is there; crinkled and dying,
grey, lifeless and gasping for air,
each time, a tragedy to share.
Suddenly, the reason for living; laid bare.

René, Brighton 2002

Waiting for Terror

So, is this the moment,
or will it be the next?
In a crowded train somewhere
where bodies come in droves,
packed into tubes like sardines,
side by side, for maximum effect.

Maybe gas, released into vents of air
will cause the throat to choke,
clutching and retching from unseen mists
that only cockroaches miss

and fell even men with sturdy trunks,
to wither under such a deadly cloak.

It will be quick when it happens, no fear!
Unless anthrax, plague or pox
comes in by stealth, on ill driven winds,
finding weak systems or stricken lungs;
poor examples of life amongst many,
already predestined for the axe.

We'll go down like flies,
as they did at Agincourt
and Mons, or with the Impi hordes.
The message then was clear

knowing full well the cause,
but waiting for terror on the 8.02
on a dull December day

is just a bore – a terrible bore.

René, London 2002

Conversations in the Wilderness

I talk to myself but no one listens,
Roller-coaster conversations
Arguments venting spleen.
Is this reality or a dream?

A neurosis founded on great fear;
Of insecurity and non-acceptance here.
There was a time when I stood alone,
As foreign as a standing stone.

Such desperation to succeed,
Maimed by doubts that impede,
Causes chaos to the bowel;
It churns in disgust.

No answers found – or none I can trust.

René, Brighton 2003 and 2006

Why Can't They See?

Is it me? Am I alone? Is anybody there?
Voices chase my brain as spectres shadow men.
A thousand clanging bells sound warnings
in ever increasing decibels,
but still no answers found, nor given.

Why can't they see the truth, like me?
A million shop-front dummies stand and stare
in 'Busby Berkley' rows of kitsch;
their vacant eyes are everywhere, but see nothing,
as rigor mortis engulfs their bloodless limbs.

I scream, why can't you see, you imbeciles –
you dolts that drag your feet in indecisive mode,
and disregard all signals given
by bards and wise men full of ken.
My faith in man in ruins – the dummies win.

René, Brighton 2004

Nightmare in Narnia?

The nightmare returns that haunts from stratosphere:
It absorbs the soul into the *avant hier*,
Where my visions of the yesteryear appear
To leave me clammy, cold with fear.

As if, through Narnia's open wardrobe door
I feel that I have passed here once before
Along dank corridors of fungal spore
Perhaps, some bloody battlefield of war?

The body has gone; only spirit remains,
An imperceptible footprint, left as a stain,
The raven pecks at a remaining grain
And I am left to face the continuing pain.

René, London-Brighton-London 2006

All Words Mean Something

What we write we mean,
Or do we?

Sometimes, always, never,
Definitively, ambiguously;
To be taken at face value,
Misinterpreted or misunderstood,
With slight or innuendo.

A dilemma for those who read
The unconnected messages of man.

René, Brighton 2006

Five Minutes to Ten

There's a baby in his gut
Churned by fear of being cut;
Been there before but not like this
All on account of too much piss.

Unease is born and long gestated
Unbirthed 'til time and vengeance sated,
Enough to form another scar
Concealing still the demon's star.

Remember when E. J. the Tub
Was rubbished at the Peak Down pub,
How stood around as in a flock
His mates did laugh at such a mock?

And even more, the famous drubbing
Were Chilla's dues from mental scrubbing
At a place of late night drinking
By Camperdown one evening's sinking?

This time it seems there might be trouble
And dickhead's for it, trouble double,
Serve him right the dipso fool
Waters broken, font's a'drool.

Chris, Mount Eliza 1993

Whose Business?

'Why do you assert me?
Tell me only what you think I meant
Or what I ought to mean
Or even what is wrong or right with me:
But do not expect me to tell you anything
That's my business not yours.'

Chris, Sydney 1995

Time

The Run

Upon a cliff top where sea birds soar,
Each morning I take flight
To pit against age and its ever closing door,
The battle never won: a constant fight.
In extreme conditions, or simply sublime,
The body is willed against time.

And when the wind shrieks and all Hell is let loose,
Not even the gulls enjoy,
As the sea unleashes its fury like some demented sluice,
Was it also like this when at Troy?
What little survives on cliff tops so bare,
Gets eaten by rabbits that come out, when they dare.

But come rain or shine, the cliff top is a haven
For reflection and time to unwind,
And like the Tower, will collapse without raven.
The views and the vistas help keep open mind,
Taking strides, reaching out, for what reason?
For the sake of my health: I am a man for all seasons.

God, how I love desolation and quiet;
Pounding feet set up rhythms I hum.
Not a soul to be seen, nor to invite;
Only once in a while a beach bum.
It's a fright and a scare when we meet there at dawn,
Me in bright singlet and he with wide yawn.

It's the pain that I love; it gives strength to go on.
I'm a masochist: it's true really true.
For the blood does pump red, not insipid nor wan,
Not cold like the sea, nor the colour of blue.
Whoever gives in or may simply wane,
Will fade in a fog of disdain.

Upon a cliff top where sea birds soar,
Each morning I take flight.
It's been ten long years, fast approaching a score,
I've thought of the world and I've thought of man's plight.
I've lived my whole life upon flint, rock and chalk,
A dedicated journey from which I'll not baulk.

René, Brighton 2001
On training for the London Marathon

Now Boys Again

These men; bald, grey and lime –
with others who have stood the test of time,
stare across a crowded room
straining to find those they knew as boys
in a time, long ago, when guns were their toys.

A wheelchair glides by; can that be Chuck?
"Say you remember when the cookhouse blew up".
There's pathos here as they cling to the past,

of memories that blind or awake in the night
but now come alight when they serve to unite.

Now boys again, together they share
moments sublime and moments to scare,
in a camp, on a mountain,
in a land often railed,
to discover 40 years on
that this bond has not failed.

René, Brighton 2004
Following the first reunion on 3 April at Tywyn, of the All Arms Junior Leaders Regiment since its and closure in 1966 (formed 1959); based at a bleak camp called Tonfanau in then Merionethshire (now Gwynedd) close to the town of Towyn (now Tywyn)

Going Nowhere Fast

Jumping on and jumping off,
Tubes that go round and round,
Like sand worms through the dunes,
Sapping our lives away;
Questioning our sanity.

Catching buses, riding trains
A taxi in between.
These are our treadmills –

Taking us everywhere,
Ending up nowhere.

René, Brighton 2006

Paging Miss Chia

'Where has this bloody year gone,
What do we do with these days
So unremarked by memory?
Where have all my lunchtimes gone?'

We commit our days to diaries,
As the mad are sent to the bin.
In hock to time is the spirit of each,
Redemption depending on you.

Diary gives back your days only
On your promise of doing its bidding,
As the asylum doors are opened only
When wild spirits are converted to sanity.

It's not just a matter of regretting their loss,
After feeding your days to a diary devouring;
Heed my call to be wary of madness
In doing to others what it's doing to you.

Chris, Singapore 1993

Jogging a Kowloon Promenade

Along the towpath of a bay
I raced a sand barge, break of day,
Red rusty was its poop and stern,
Chug-chugging sweetly miles to burn.

No human face or movement seen
On board that carrier serene,
Merely a pile of yellow sand
Amidships loaded, bound for land.

What if it were not us who sped,
But ground and sea, together wed,
As on life's treadmill pounded hard,
Reality and truth disbarred?

What if the barge and I were whirled,
Within a spinning stilling world,
And at its centre, mute and bound
We're strung together, souls aground?

Perhaps we ran at hopeless speed
Just like a harried centipede,
Whose limbs galore elide its fear
The head ahead to race the rear?

Like sand, though burden to the boat,
Makes its economics float,
Reason, as ballast to our dreams
Is counterweight to much that seems.

Chris, Hong Kong 1993

Two Late

In time they trooped into the room,
Quite scant their hair, and dun their minds;
Old soldiers waiting on their doom,
Old men whose meets are yearly finds.
And now the talk's of worn-dry plots,
(But careful of their zones no go)
From one of Albion's hot flung spots,
Great deeds accomplished long ago.
Hang on! Two oddballs in their midst,
One dark of eye one light of hair,
Talk sourly of the verbal mist
Which shrouds the misfit's quest for flair.
Relieved, they turn to leave the place,
Find refuge from the Janus face.

Chris, La Chaise-Dieu 2002

War

With God on Our Side

The crusade has begun
against terror and strife.
It's good against evil,
America has the right
to take righteous action.
It's so easy to decide
when action is justified,
with God on their side.

Do not speak of Allah,
nor Palestine either,
but, of Israeli settlers
so upright and true,
who stole Arab lands.
On the US they relied;
how can it be wrong,
with God on their side?

Oh, the gun is a killer;
worshipped by all in the States,
but as a terrorist weapon,
it bears all the wrong traits.
Americans simply can't see it,
in their bunkers they hide;
to fight the next war,
with God on their side.

So, with lethal injection,
and by electric chair,
they kill one another
without compunction, or care.
It's called capital punishment;
it's well tested and tried
in God's own country,
with God on their side.

And, the world it is global,
for to plunder and loot.
To manipulate and take over,
for new culture to root.
Here comes the new empire;
all others deride.
All bow to the dollar,
with God on its side.

God bless America,
and God Bless My Mom.
We'll rid the world of terror,
we'll just bomb, bomb, bomb.
It's a premise bound to fail,
'cause terror it will hide
and return again one day,
with God on its side.

René, Brighton 2002
Based on Bob Dylan's 'With God on Our Side' 1963

21st Century Paradox

One million starve in Africa
where despots go to war.
Whichever way, it's massacre.
not for the rich, but poor.
Others die in needless pain,
with squalor and filth around.
They have no hope, expect no gain:
the dispossessed abound.
Not far away lie cities of greed
where obscene wealth is flaunted.
It's here where despots feed,
their appetites undaunted.

Such inequality is like a pox,
a 21st century paradox.

René, Brighton 2002

Brambles in the Hedgerows

In a village compound
hope hangs limp,
as anarchy sets its stall
in a jungle brawl.

Life ebbs away,
as a mango falls,
butchered like a pig on a stick,
for birds of prey to pick.

Root crops fail
amid the dusty fields
devoid of life and shrivelled dry,
where the seed will shy.

Young die fat
with pregnant bellies of air
and limpid eyes accepting fate:
these are brambles in the hedgerows
that tear at passers-by.

René, Brighton 2003

Wellington's Injunction

Now fire at will, you Tommies brave,
Four-square you've been against the French,
Repulsed the pride of wave on wave
Of Boney's best who pile in stench.

Four-square you've been against the French,
You steadfast redcoats press the brave

Of Boney's best who pile in stench
Not one of whom can us enslave.

You steadfast redcoats press the brave,
Whose chargers by their riders lay
Not one of whom can us enslave.
No more of pretty Paris gay,

Whose chargers by their side do lay
A bloody mess is their enclave,
No more of pretty Paris gay.
Now fire at will, you Tommies brave.

Chris, Ampthill 2010

Footprints

Followers of the Fox's Path

They came from far and wide –
young boys in their prime,
as their fathers and grandfathers
had come before them,
seeking a place in history
with fife and drum and duty bound.
Tonfanau Halt, 'twixt sea and Fox's Path
was the start and end of their journey,
where canny Scot met West Country crew
and the Ulster lilt sang with the Geordie few
and the Cockney lad scoffed at the Scouser's brew
but once past the gate, the language was blue.
This camp; condemned by others long before,
when shells still fell on hallowed ground,
lay yet to prepare for war; to carry flags to the end,
imbued by a discipline so severe
that drove to cut off toe or puncture ear,
as boy soldiers learnt what there was to fear.
Armed with green ponchos and ill-fitting boots
Cader Idris and the Plynlimon Hills were assaulted.
Hell and high water was repelled, at a cost
when the blood from ones eyelets started seeping
and as skin became blue from the freezing –
and where sheep, ever present, kept on bleating.
Inside the billets nightly stories regaled,
warmed by the stoves of Satan himself

boys played with bayonets like darts on a board.
The bull never stopped nor was ignored:
the spit and polish like broken record,
then trashed in the morning – sergeant had scored!
Until that final moment, so surreal and sublime,
on a parade ground of cold and steel,
when boys became men at the going down of the sun
to the bugle's 'Last Post' and a life yet to come,
as the train sped away to new lands so far flung
that could end like a fox – at the end of gun.

René, Brighton 2003
On time as a boy soldier in Tonfanau, Wales

And Did Those Feet…?

Tread upon ancient ground, old as Jerusalem;
Trample Earth's crust, extruded from life;
Trudge through mud more organic than Mars;
Traipse across Downland in shadows long-fallen?

Wince from flint, honed sharp by the Gods;
Walk in pain – claiming no sympathy or respite;
Weave above the Weald, beacons to all below;
Wind an unrelenting journey towards infinity?

Travel such distance that dulled rational thought;
Transcend time through endorphins of the mind;

Track sheep and hare that stayed, not like us;
Trail-blaze to question our mortality, once more?

René, Brighton 2004

The Big Walk

This bond, kept intact through two score years
Is put to the test once more
On England's Downs, always there to divide,
Where more ups and downs abide.

This walk, shared by many others before,
Allows mind, body and spirit to flow
As ghosts of the past catch up with the present
Through an earth rich and nascent.

Let the elements be the judges
Of such feeble a pair
That dare to challenge the Gods
As they take to the land to rekindle the odds.

René, Brighton 2004

Messages from Under Foot

Walking the trammelled paths of yesteryear –
Faint lines that track across the land,
Aside a waterway, atop a ridge
Aflame with sun and pounded by rain,
I feel as one with those before me
That journeyed oxen carts by day and night
To market weekly precious fare
Or maypole dance the rites of spring,
That watched their sons, as soldiers, leave
To never return for harvest time.

And, as I tread those same worn ruts,
For other reasons now than then,
I sense their presence under foot,
As in haste, they fled marauding bands
Saving their daughters from ravaging hands
And, leaving traces of their lives behind,
They left forever for distant lands.

Through flint and chalk they speak to me
Of pain and suffering and hardship too
But, of a similar love of the land they knew.

René, Brighton 2007

Snow Simile

What is it to meet your snowprints facing?
As looking in a mirror, toe to toe,
But this image you can pass through
And out the other side
Like a ghost.

Fearful, wheel half-circle to
Assume again your self

In which you would rather
Have left well alone
The burdensome reciprocal.

Chris, Oundle 2004

Natter

About old Druids' meeting rings.
About what mind and body brings
About this Sussex winter walk.
About a hearty dearth of talk
About our service for the Queen.
About our lustrous issues keen

About a youth disintegrated
About a life pontificated.

Chris, Oundle 2004

South Downs Way

Beside a blasted stump at Chanctonbury Ring
We lunched to stay the cold and wet.
It was, we agreed, the best of times to be,
Together against the mother of all weather.

Anxiously behind the mist, the sun hid herself,
Stopped the marvel of English patchwork,
Dulled the brilliance of teardrops from the twig,
And dried not even a bit of our gear.

What we could do though, was to share a piece of
German-tasting shop cake, which his wife had made him
Cut into daft little pieces whose crumbs played about
His fingers like Blake's grains.

Chris, Oundle 2004

Roots

Sepia

In awe and with fascination strong,
I look at the sepia of the long gone.
Untold moments and secret lives,
Creased and crinkled like disposed wives.

Faded, wan, unreal, distant;
Images of people and places extant.
Who cares for them now; in this bright new age,
Where sepia is forgotten, no more to engage?

But, from sepia we can learn
Why others they did burn:
How life, lived in the past,
Helped to strengthen the mast.

Wistful faces peer out from within:
They too faced decisions of how to begin.
Human emotion; unchanged but redirected.
They loved and they lived and they always expected.

Whole generations entombed side by side;
In albums of sepia, hiding colours of pride.
Love does not reside with only those of today:
Strong emotions and valour; caused them also to pray.

So cast not aside, nor ignore
Our own forebears of yore:

For the sepia we want to declaim,
Will soon become our own constant refrain.

René, BA to Geneva 2001

Roots

Continental Europe pulls unseen,
Where Huguenot stock still clean,
Sail azure lakes 'gainst virgin snow;
Remind me of kin, so long ago.

What life led they then,
In small families of ten,
When Franz Josef was King,
And children would sing?

They haunt me and stare
From those albums so fair,
Roots from all races:
Questions on their faces.

Do souls emanate from stones,
Where once lay their bones?
Do visions appear from nowhere:
Those not known, laid bare?

Clusters of villages, lives intertwined;
Feuds, strife and rituals, often designed.

Proud fathers, toiling fierce to provide:
Mothers bear children for all to survive.

From Swiss pastures they left for new land:
Two brothers and an adventure in Saskatchewan;
To Prague, went others and to London still more,
But in Konigsberg, Prussia, it ended in war.

When hurtling through Europe by passenger train,
Flashbacks and images repossess my brain.
Still there in small villages, I know
The ghosts of my past tap my shoulder, 'Hello'.

Some frittered vast wealth, played 'La vie en rose';
Gambling, debauchery, how well Bacchus knows.
Not knowing the future nor caring a fig,
They rode themselves out astride fate and a pig.

Others lived lives to the glory of God:
Protestant true and Catholic zealot,
The same guidance they sought but in churches apart,
Very few joined together, in affairs of the heart.

At the end of the day when life has passed by,
We all have to leave, we all have to die.
But the roots still remain, so strongly embedded
Across lands far and wide, where my family have ended.

By René, Brighton 2001
On his family history

Graffiti Bandits!

This **blight**, made in dead of night,
swathes of silver sheen and *Day-Glo Red*
scream ZAG and **RAZ** within our sight,
pock marks of vulgarity mar each turn.

An endless track exists to **strafe**
and spray or scrawl in *alien* script.
No pole, nor fence, or sign is safe:
we question why? No answers given.

So let *vigilantes* loose at night
with equally urban habits
and, infrared AK47 sights
to rid us of *Graffiti Bandits!*

René, Brighton 2005

This England

This England

Engraved by furrows of urban sprawl
Where blighted shop fronts mar our view,
And Saturday night drowns in vomit,
As spray cans speak in trackside code;

A chronic pox that spreads after dark,
Leaving their marks as ugly scars
Still casts a spell

When bluebells first emerge.

René, Brighton 2005 and 2006

73 Whitepit Lane

She's bought now, three-up and three-down,
A place of rest for them, Mount Joy beckoning,
And what do I ponder on, now for me at home?

Will they rage at night, their aging feuds extended,
Or will they be at peace, one for the other?
I think they still will battle, so I wish each equal might.

This land is dry this year, hot winds sweep the trees,
Fires rage inland; the soil has boils,
But it's for England I weep, full of Mum and Dad and me.

I cry for her soft rain, for her low leaden sky,
And the green grass, soothing my unshod sole,
And those shillings of bathwater grudgingly poured.

I have seen her, like the smudge on the horizon
Passing from the castaway, insult to his plight,
Quite still to the eye, a trick of disappearance.

That's what I think, that she'll always be there:
A Mother to be called; a church bell pealing.
Only there it is, and here I am.

Chris, Hunters Hill 1994
On his parents' new home; Mount Joy is a cemetery

Parallax

Bourneville Plain at sixpence a bar,
Mild brimming a mucky froth,
Unpantied girls' romp with Hemmings,
A new wife, buttered toast, broke.
Farewell to old England.

A friend pokes fun at my
Memories, says I wear the
Rose-coloured glasses of the fretful
Émigré, says I have no rights
Not even to the toast.

Botany Bay beneath me falls away
A memory lens-worn
Giving and lending and yielding

Now a firmer set of expectations
Of a new way of doing time.

Not resurrection, no third-day job,
No disturbing the ashes of a burnt-out case
Cooked as this morning's New England
Landscape, ulcerous, dry, mocking:
More of a new thing old thing.

When nostalgia crammed the spirit
People like him were right, but never
Was the idea wrong – the idea of
England in my head, unhinged
By old-fashioned hankering.

Now it is like how you overcome
Parallax and it takes
Effort to get the eye and mind to agree
The point of intersection
Where your love is finally clear.

Chris, BA 10 to London 2004

Loving Old Wisdens

Books of ancient binding
Ready for the reading
Waiting for the wenching
Caressing of the covers

On limp yellowed letters,
Fingers all a flutter,
Panting like a paddler
Cleaving her canoe.

On the pages parting
Shall we have the shudder:
Furied fancy frisson
Nicely needing nulling?

Chris, Ampthill 2008

Treadmills

Train Opus

Who are
These people
Alien to me
In Armani suits
With no ties
Next to girls
In glitter
With thongs
That ride
Above the bum
Stepping on and off
This satellite train
Wearing this and that
Staring into space
Not knowing what they see
Their thoughts to themselves
Passing messages with their thumbs?

René, Brighton 2006
Commuting, Brighton to London

Scrap Heap Blues

Normal day, as always –
      Same train, same people
Taking in the view, as you do
      'Another day another dollar', as they say
Checking what is new.

The search for excellence continues
      There are KPIs on which to report
To check you're still on the ball
      To tell if you're only just cruising
And how long before you must fall.

'Cause change is a-coming
      Efficiency is king
The man with a plan is arriving
      He sure as Hell has one for you
It's wham bam and thank you Ma'am
      Time to move on, it's true.

René, Brighton 2008
Following redundancy

Courage at the End of the Conference

There's not a dry eye in the house,
The shifting throng bids last bye byes.
Above them on the high catwalk, a
Ponderous lion paces,
Slit-eyes glittering at
His feast to come.

Jolly good, oh my eye, last goodbye,
Moves the herd towards the door.
A ghostly, sharp-clawed paw pats
The members on the head, feeling
Meat and bones.

Outstanding plans! Stuff of watersheds!
Disperse the flock to start the work.
Silken, silently, walking within them frets
The worry that even gazelles give greater chase
Before they're eaten.

Chris, Singapore 1992

Waiting for Roy

Soon we'll get started
Our words'll be shuffled,
Believing in the day
Believing in my pay.

Spreadeagled on a wall chart,
Their virginity bled.
Believing in the day
Believing in my pay.

Add a third dimension
Which lights the idea dread
Believing in the day
Believing in my pay.

That the chart is but a mirror,
Gazing on us, dead,
Believing in its day
Believing in our pay.

Chris, Singapore 1994

The Train

There are too many people on this train
Beating up to London back to the sea,
Through dark suburbs hard by the city lain.
Fast packed, no room for a flea:
Some skim the daily pulp;
Another nods at empty fields;
Some a cup of coffee gulp;
And one a nostrilled finger wields.
And I, askance at the mêlée,
Plod the ritual of my pen
Which tells me, writing, to belay
Brighton, entrained, once again,
Too, too many of us hurtling
To another day belittling.

Chris, Singapore 2002

Love

The Initiation

Schnapps
at high altitude
sets the blood pumping
ready,
for when toboggans set off,
cursing
through pine.

Schnapps
fuelling spirit and frame,
flying through space,
holding on
for dear life with
intoxicating speed,
driving man against planet.

Feet
out akimbo,
rudders of flesh.
Steering, ploughing,
through snow, earth and cones,
screaming Devil may care,
living just for the moment.

Endorphins release
all the way;
we're racing for life,
for the race must be won:
There's a pride and desire

to be first,
to succeed.

Success
must be ours
and, none can be better
than Matthew and I,
united
as one team,
unspoken.

Others
passed by,
left behind in a blur
in the pitch that is night,
derailed
and detracted,
as they flounder and flail.

Flotsam
and jetsam,
they lie strewn all around;
behind us a melee
of error and despair,
of faulty tactics;
of insufficient care.

René, Bad Kleinkirchheim, Austria 1988
Midnight toboggan ride under the influence of schnapps,
with son Matthew

Unspoken

Across the table, in curls,
That swirl in time with the sea,
Golden kissed with sprays of light,
Sits an angel with anemone eyes,
Where limpid pools of blue
Reflect from unknown space.

And lips so perfectly formed
In pink and ready to kiss,
That cause a man to lose
His self-control, his cool,
As imagination raises the heat
And anvils pound to the beat.

Soft skin
Anticipates the hand
That brings a coarseness with it
Relentless, finding its way
With unspoken certainty –
Needing no explanation.

René, Brighton 2006

Summit

What drives our need
To reach new heights
Into the thinning air
And pinnacles in the sky
When lungs and limbs propel
To battle the pencil piste
With crags that jut
In hues of darkness
And give no truck
To those who fail?

To pit against such forces
When the bosom folds
Of the land below
Fade at every turn
Force questions to be asked
But, answers rarely found,
Where Alpine choughs glide by
As sirens, beckoning on,
I thought I heard them cry
For those who died before us.

Ignored, we carried on
Into the great white void
Where the summit lies.

Once found, never satisfied.

René, Brighton 2015
Following his ascent of Mont Blanc

Decibel Love

She says
It's the way that I talk to her,
The way I look at her,
She says I look as if something's wrong.
I say, 'No I'm fine, really.'
She doesn't believe me.
I don't understand why.
She gets angry;
Tells me I never listen;
That she's told me a thousand times before.
I stay calm, too calm for her.
She gets annoyed at how calm I am,
Much too calm for her.
She thinks, what is he so calm about?
So I explode and make her angry.
She thinks, why can't he control himself?
We scream at each other;
Say awful things.
Our faces turn red and the air turns blue.
She storms out of the room;
I shout abuse after her.
I hear her cry and mutter in the kitchen.
I continue to storm and curse her stupidity.
We both fall silent,
Each to our own damaged thoughts.
Eventually, I make her a cup of tea
And, countdown to the next time
We show our love for each other.

René, Brighton 2006

Here Today, Gone Tomorrow

He was here, just now, just a second ago;
confident in his quiet assertive way,
making strides on his stairway to success –
in command of his destiny.

Now he's gone; what's left is a void
that impels me to plunge right in,
where the mind is numb and the voice is dumb
and nothing seems the same.

He was here, just now, by my side;
my son, with whom I grew,
laughing and doing things boys love to do:
It seems only yesterday we spent a day at the zoo.

But now he is gone, so far away
in a place that's stark and wild,
making history as we speak,
taking chances, as you do.

He was here, just now, not long ago
as we talked about the war,
taking all for granted, as we did.
seeking out adventures new.

I like to think I gave him love
and a zest for life to be lived.
I like to believe that he loved me too
and remembers our day at the zoo.

Now, his room stands waiting:
a chapel to all he holds dear
with mementoes brought from far and wide;
where only his return is unsure.

He was here, just now, being strong before he went
but, I wondered how strong I would be,
left to explain to the animals on his shelf,
also waiting – but not for me.

René, Brighton 2003–2006
On his son's departure and time in Afghanistan working for
the United Nations

Cold Flame

Long past its run,
Our lightness, near to out,
Meets a darker radiance
Of terror stalking
Our strangling longings,
Plucking the strings of our
Hopeless gyres.

You move a way I
Do not know its dangers
Or its pleasures,
I know only that this division
Of journeys is right
And we shall glow
For all our failing lights.

Like a sputtering candle flame
It seems to warm so cold,
Must not defile,
But cauterise;
For, as the wick is
Sacrificed in fire and air
So perhaps our pyre becomes us.

Chris, Sydney 1993

Twenty-first Birthday

Now you're twenty-one, JK,
We hope you'll find your own true way,
And beat the tympani of life
According to your joy and strife.
      You've come a long way, JK,
  Since you were a babee.

We'll shed a tear of gratitude
Because you are a real good dude;
We've heard it won't be very long
Before you join the worldly throng.
      You've come a long way, JK,
  Since you were a babee.

You must forgive a line or two
Of reference to some ancient blue:
For instance, whom the cubby torched
And was at Clark's Point debauched?
Remember also Lima lady
A mere three bucks for action shady!
And not to mention cars all wrecked
But that's a topic we'll not select.
      You've come a long way, JK,
  Since you were a babee.

Now as a film man working free
Makes you happy we'll agree.
We hope that you will ever see
Dreams fulfilled and peacefully.
      You've come a long way, JK,
  Since you were a babee.

Chris, Hunters Hill 1994
Blue: Austr. slang for disagreement

Hot Gums

Two lemon-scented gums
Wave frantically at each other
Bending to the hot westerly

Their trunks in unison.
Their branches not.

Chris, Hunters Hill 1994

Lunch

At lunch, as I sit and watch, I
Could say,
'You are clutched and shoved
By a wild thing which only you can see:
It muffles your heart
It deadens your eyes
It unsweetens your words.
You do your weeping at your sink,
A tea-towel dangling from a hand,
A girl-child's eyes wide and wondering upon you;
Not here where your struggle is so evident. Like
The dinner-time gawp at Bosnia's screen of misery,
The place for me is in the imagined pain.'
But I won't, will I?

Now, your sideways glance from a grey eye,
Tries my interest to respond,
And your heart your eyes your mouth all smile together,
To make lunch like it was once, a little.

Chris, Hunters Hill 1995

Apple Tree Bay to Berowra

Past banked and close-knit blackboys, we stride the
Waterside track and 'look!' below at
Fishy shapes which swish in shoals unmuddied
From rainless days on end and end.

Green droplets of berries droop an unnamed bush near
Where the sun is a cool stranger, bracken grows surprising
      green
In the darkness visible along the shadow of a small bay's vee
Across which we scramble and slide on rock slime with a
      green less so.

We stop, and feel the river's
Still and sparkling gaze
Quieten us two
As one.

Chris, Hunters Hill 2004

Castello di Uzzano

Beside the vines she sat him,
Crumpled as his crumpled canvas hat
That warded off the stifling heat of
Afternoon in the castle of his dreams.

Presently, boys came with red apples in a basket,
Milling a little beside him, their quiet voices
In the rustling of the hanging leaves
Salving his wild within.

He gazed on the quad of gravel,
Heard the Algerian's crippled tread
Make towards the room of wines
Where she had taken her retreat.

The apple-eaters soon fell away
And the whole fell silent
Except for the moans of pigeons
High, unseen in the porticoes.

After the sun was evening-cooled,
The two ate quietly on cold cuts,
Bought earlier before the telling
Of her truth of why they both were there.

At night their dreams were of others
Loved or cared about or borne.

But in the morning cool and light, they
Lay close, murmured to and of each other.

Chris, Sydney 1999

A Melbourne Park

They picnicked under occasional sun.
Swan wings flapped against a child's fear,
A man, head down, wrote out notes.
Seagulls pecked each other and hapless fowls.

A quiet woman bent to the water,
Looked in a book and back again
To check her child. Then they
Watched her raise a brolly to the rain.

Presently, the drizzle stopped and low sun
Shafts hued the grass a gaudy green.
Two pied lovebirds darted 'Look!'
But she missed their blink-proof flight.

Later, away from the lake and higher,
They wandered a garden of decaying
Blooms, until their steps and hearts
Moved unwilling to the gate.

Chris, South Yarra 2001

Death

Tempus Fugit

Turning the corner, I see him there,
eyes closed, waiting for the end;
a man I do not know –
yet knew all my life,
now reduced to this,

My eyes become a sea –
through the brine I see him still,
chasing, whooping, laughing,
crashing through Spring woods,
the Uncle I once knew.

If you could have seen him,
as I did then,
on a death bed that sapped his last;
where worms had had their way,
I begged, "Don't Go" –

But he does, and his going
takes a part of me with him,
of a life shared, full of fun,
of simple adventures,
that first appalling camper's stew,

This is what I remember him by,
And, as I do, my body rocks
from spasms of loss and grief –
sobs that rip apart the soul,

a hurt not known or felt before,
angry and confused.

But what I will never forget
were his eyes, shut throughout,
Oblivious to my expression of grief;
to the love that I felt and the loss,
when all I wanted to do, but could not,
was to have whispered 'Goodbye.'

René, Brighton 2004
On the death of Peter, his favourite uncle

Picking up His Baton

One thousand chandeliers
In the grand hotels of Europe's best
Dipped on August 4;
Each finely cut crystal pendant –
A reflection of the many facets of his life –
Twinkled as it faded.
One thousand orchestras are still:
Only echoes of their music remain;
Of lilting strains and joyous pomp;
Of myths and legends and operatic plots
Where Romeo met his Juliet
And Siegfried his Brunhilde.
One thousand chefs have stopped

Their master crafts in culinary art
With Larousse by their side
In the shadow of Escoffier
In the pursuit of perfection
Born of love and devotion.
One thousand poets recite no more,
Odes of romance and chivalry
Where reality is put aside
For dreams to be created
To reach another level
Where anything is possible.
Now, two families mourn
But, four brothers reunite,
And Czech ancestors stir
As dew forms in a Swiss valley:
In England, his baton for conducting life
Is finally passed on, and accepted, with love and dignity.

René, Woodvale Crematorium Chapel, Brighton 2005
Four days after the death of his father, read by him at the
cremation service

A Frail Eternity

And still, as the dark side of the moon appears,
Sweet rays of light revive the necessary zest
To carry on the Olympian resolve, to not give up,
To bear the trials and tribulations of life

On pitted paths of unknown destination,
Oft' blurred by fogs of fear,
Where baited traps await us.

This thing called age confounds us all,
As some fade fast, like autumn leaves,
Whilst others find reserves of sap
Helping feed the withering trunk;
And, in some far corner of the brain,
Exists the will to power us on,
Beyond all doubt.

But, even this, in time, will surrender its hold
On ageing sinew that turns to mulch, then dust.
Before that day, heed the wonderment of life;
The miracles of butterfly and bee,
And spiders that spin in silk and symmetry –
With webs that glisten in early morning dew,
And share with us this frail eternity.

René, Brighton 2005

From Weimar, with Love

A German church, silent, Rococo.
'Why do I talk to a ghost?
How dare you lie in heaven
Rather than sulk on earth!

What right, had you to break
The yarns between us?'
Stonily, a gargoyle's stare returns.

'Have you seen my Dad?' a
Call to me the Friday
We hoped to meet, sit and talk of
Words and women,
Of sons and Satan,
Of us, thirty-odd years known.
But he didn't turn up, did Gerry,

An out-of-joint Augustan,
Secreting moralising couplets:
'Seer', 'Remorse', 'Erred'.
Beard yellow from shag,
Teeth in faggots, limbs at odds with cane,
White hair fringing a fissured brow.
Found dead in his shed on the third day.

I mourn for him as I would a woman:
The might-have-beens
Untouchable, forbidden as the
Gold in this exquisite tapestry.

Chris, Wyegate Green 2002

Samaritans' Nightshift

Was it just the murmuring to the handset
Are you still there, I'm on your side, I'm here for you
That I remember of his four-hour vigil for her
Who ebbed until the wee hours' dawn
Lit a hand limp beside his coffee cold?

A long question, eh? But not as long as the living murk of
Dad and friends' dread games with girl-child
Whose ever, ever absence from that world of pain
Sullies all of us left merely tired, bereft,
Wondering if those gifts of ear and mouth calmed death.

Chris, Clayton West 2005

Mates

Friendship

It doesn't come lightly, nor even free;
it cannot be gained over teacakes and tea;
a lifetime can pass, with nothing to see
but when it arrives; lasts endlessly.

It readily accepts both foibles and faults,
in adversity and trouble; exalts,
that gnawing state of loneliness; it halts,
helping old soldiers and even old salts.

It means understanding; no words being said,
no time required, getting inside the head;
and still there, even after time has sped,
knowing it remains, long after you're dead.

René, Brighton 2002

The Rakes' Progress

From Southwark streets, devoid
Of those who cared how once they looked
Scarred by hurried plans –
And, blurred of any vision,
Step by step they found
A trace of Dickens' past.

The passing time ferments
In draughts of yeast, the reason why,
Still now, they tread byways –
Mere shadows of their past
In debt to Marshalsea
Until the Rake is seen.

The paradox was clear
As the bell continued to toll
Counting down a dull brain –
The pretty things were out
To celebrate new world
Of cocktail froth surreal.

René, Brighton 2008

Emotional Pasta

Across the viaduct, astride the City,
Far enough from their comfort zones,
They rode to Lewes to face their fears;
To muse again their fading lives;
And defer to their respective wives.

In Arenas where men with beards
Sat cornered with ale, and mute,
The contest began, as it had before,

Of parry and thrust, to head and heart
Until, once more; time to depart.

The Castle Tower was left – it mattered not;
The books of old – still there to review,
Dull people with comfortable lives
Swirled and busied in their own way,
Unaware of emotional pasta experienced that day.

René, Brighton, Lewes 2009
With Chris in Lewes

Meeting at Boat Quay

It's a furnace of a day for walking
Along the river's edge but
Keeping to the shade of awnings
Past Chinese, Indian, Italian, Thai
Shop houses, all empty at ten to three,
Except for sullen clumps of waiters
Waiting their weary evenings to begin.

And inside Harry's, cool, empty
With cigarettes and Tiger,
Both burning bright.
But not as bright as she,
Her smile and folded knee.

Well are we met!
Three months!
Really!
Can it be as long?
What do you have for me?
Look what I have for you!
And you!

Books and journals shuffle between
Our smiles and looks and grins and winks
Until we end up with the same amount.

At Molly Malone's (another cool place)
A pisshead Aussie in paunchy shorts
Calls her wife, then girlfriend,
But we settle on friend.
At last, when he falls away, we talk
Of familiar, untidy things,
Flitting between shambling mental rooms
Drained of living and loving,
Leaving no trace of ourselves.

Outside, hatted to the heat,
We said goodbye,
And walked apart,
Our exchanges resting
In tight-clutched bags.

Chris, Singapore and Sydney 1996

Misfits Redux

In from Brighton and
Ampthill, two old soldiers to
London to drink. Southwark tube on a
Chill cold day, glove and scarf against the
Wind under a happy, blue, December sky.

By midday, a heart-starter, an IPA half to begin
Talk of work, women and themselves:
One full of latter-day post-corporate fluff, the other
Blasé, clutching a guide to inns that survived the bombs.
In the Truman's pub one beery seer intones 'The Rake,
Unmissable,' so is added to the route. Around
From the Charles Dickens, the Marshalsea is a mere
Forgotten wall with a reluctant council plaque.
In the darkling, later, they break from the
Route eying the glittering sweep from
The Gherkin to St Paul's: a city sequinned.
East of The Borough, they hurry down drinkless streets
Chasing one's leathered ancestry: here a
Resurrected memory, there,
A stab at what might have been for the tanning dead. In
The oracle's add-on, a motley
Press of jabbering youngsters and our heroes bend to
Paradox – micro-brewed, dark
Sweet ten per cent of devilry –
Apparent nonsense that becomes a current truth of
Present pleasure and tomorrow's dreams.

On late trains home from London Bridge
These grey-haired boys leave
Behind more memories
Than are to come.
Sobering.

Chris, Ampthill 2008

An Afternoon's Drinking

To some it is beyond the pale
Before midday to drink an ale
To sink the foaming amber brew,
'The sides untouched – the same for you?'

That's how it starts on this sunny Lewes
Day. Our first pub swarms with
Silvery-permed women clutching oversized
Menus beside obedient portly husbands.

Next, at a napped-flint drinker's pub,
Men slot here and there beside their dogs,
One, snowy-haired, reads the *Telegraph*,
Another rests a gammy leg upon a stool.

Past Turkish baths and Henrietta's house,
Past Henry's payoff to Anne of Cleves,

A house she never sat in. Past one
Of Thomas Paine's

Delightful pubs that time forgets,
Click-clack heels on scrubbed-down deal.
Some not so fine, with students' din.
Background to a well-tilled friendship.

Lunch. 'It's where I came with Dad sometimes,
Brought him down from Rottingdean.'
Soon, he softly weeps about that dad,
But I keep mine inside my head.

Back in Brighton, we move to end
The thing up St James's Street, eat
Nasty Chinese fish and chips, looked
On by a chubby-cheeked queen in a panama.

To some it is beyond the pale
Before midday to drink an ale
To sink the foaming amber brew,
'The sides untouched – the same for you?'

Chris, Ampthill 2009

Travel

In the Deserts of this Earth

In the stillness that is deafening,
In the space that is engulfing,
In the palate rich in colour,
In the deserts of this earth,

Man is but a grain of sand,
Man is stripped of all excess,
Man is nothing more than less,
Man is impotent at best.

Time is endless, with little meaning,
Time passes by without hesitation,
Time waits for no man, nor gives explanation,
Time takes its time; simply nothing to wait for.

Alone in the desert like Beauty and the Beast,
Alone with one's fear, fermenting like yeast,
Alone with the stars; orgasmic to the eyes,
Alone with one's body; pulsating, on fire.

In the deserts of this earth
Man is laid bare

Where neither God, nor even Allah,
Gives a jot, or cares.

René, Brighton 2001
On his time in the Sahara Desert

Rainforest Man

In Lillian Rock lives Rainforest Man,
'Mongst pretty-faced wallaby and Mt Warning's span.
Cicadas pierce eardrums with their incessant sound,
Whilst brush turkeys ferret from decomposing ground.

> *33 years ago in a far distant land*
> *He was known then only as, Morocco Man.*
> *He rode ships of the desert through sand seas of dunes*
> *Driven on by lamb Tagines and Jethro Tull tunes.*

But in Lillifield, in a community fair mixed,
He builds a pole house from gums, no longer fixed.
Taken from the bush; alive day and night,
The huntsman and wolf spiders, both lie within sight.

> *'Cross Tizi 'n Test leaving dust trails behind.*
> *The Atlas, so rugged, hidden amethysts to find.*
> *Ksar-peppered river valleys, fertile with palm,*
> *Was the home of his youth, providing succour and balm.*

Now he looks out onto bush in its prime,
In a land called Gondwana, at the edge of his time.
Spangled drongo exclaim in the caldera extinct
Where his spirit has led him; enhanced by instinct.

> *Nomadic by nature; feeling at home where he lay,*
> *It took him to Merzouga and M'Hamid to play*

> *'Cross stark lunar landscapes, their beauty extreme;*
> *Shared this love of raw nature with others, his dream.*

Red-legged pademelon now awaken his day
And the kookaburra cackles in a hysterical way.
King parrots blind with colour, from dawn through to dusk:
Here, Rainforest Man grows like a seed from a husk.

René, Australia 2002
After visiting Paul Hargan in his Lillifield Community home
in Lillian Rock, NSW

The Voyage

Anticipation gnaws at the gut weeks before;
Some say wolves bay with the same intensity, and more.
Watching the clock tick by, the seconds loud and long,
Waiting for the moment in time to be gone.

>   Then comes relief,
>   Endorphin release,
>   Leave care behind,
>   Clear out the mind.
>   Beer, wine and gin,
>   Let the voyage begin.

Minutiae of preparation, agonisingly slow, now over
When you step out of door into bright green clover,

Leaving behind grey skies and ever-present cobwebs:
The shackles of routine relegated to dregs.

> Eyes open wide,
> Euphoria can't hide,
> Novel, new, afresh;
> As pleasures of the flesh.
> Sights extraordinary,
> With each new ferry.

Those facial lines drawn from life take new shape,
From frown into grin, as with prune into grape;
No need for surgery, this is therapy so pure,
Rejuvenating life for its ability to endure.

> Now open mind,
> No longer blind,
> Let visions appear.
> No need to fear,
> Reduce the mundane,
> Ignite the flame.

To decide to go is the hardest part,
But when it is done, the pulse takes heart
As the detritus of woe gets left far behind:
The voyage can begin, in another corner of the mind.

René, London to Sydney 2002
At the start of a long-anticipated holiday, after a hard and stressful year

The Lonely Guillemot of Dún na nGall

Black bog meets black crag
in wild Dún na nGall
and a billion fine grains
light yellow crescents of strand;
where bracken meets bramble
in overgrown jungles of green
and atop, patches of 'sunstone'
blind from afar,
as Errigal's peak reaches up to a star.

As the oystercatcher feeds
the curlew cries out
while rare corncrakes croak.
Golden eagles soar above Horn Head
where meadow pipits chatter through fern;
fulmars glide in circles of mist
as sandpipers pick nervously the sand
but the lonely guillemot on cliff edge so high
simply waits, for the time to pass by.

This stark landscape
hewn by the Devil, indented by time,
manicured by the hand of God;
bitter-sweet to those who set foot on it
inspires music and lyrics of contradiction.
Raw Pogues and Boomtown Rats
are tamed by Clannad's Celtic lilt

but U2 powers up, drives on acute;
not even the poet stays mute.

Such panoramas that blind
render the mind to unravel;
uncertain of reality
or comprehension of scale
sometimes clear, sometimes blurred.
Nature's amphetamines for life
kick into the tunnels of my brain
revealing the guillemot in me
looking down from above
to survey in solitude all that I see.

René, 2003
Following a week's walking and touring through Donegal

Not so Much a Street, More a Way of Life

By day alike any other;
a street with little to record
outside the grey monsoon ditch of normality
where scurrying cockroaches clitter-clatter *en masse*;
their antennae picking up the impending doom
as swathes of swirling, gurgling,
rushing torrents of water

engulf each battalion in their tidal formations
to be deposited elsewhere in smarter suburbs
or to rise again from main street manholes –
like aliens in the city.

This street, so serene by day,
transforms each night; a chameleon of life,
home to other creatures of the darker world
that blinker into light like moths around a flame,
their delicate wings in danger of burning,
to disappear in the flicker of a wing beat
plying their trade for all to see
but not what it seems and there are no rules
in the opium den, only those to be broken,
as pedlars cheat and beggars bleat, in Singapore,
in Bugis Street.

René, Brighton 2004
On Bugis Street, Singapore in 1965

Fig Andalus

Stone pueblos cluster
On Moorish Alpujarran hillsides
Lost conquests of those who came first
Newly rekindled for a new age.

At night they glow like stars
Across the valleys and ravines
Criss-crossed by *senderos*
As old as the hills.

Bearing witness to timeless skills
Perched as the Eagle will do
High above the valley below
Capturing clean water, sun and cool air.

And, on small terraces carved from the land
The olive and fig, and a harvest so pure
Provides, to be blessed by the saints
Who showed the way to follow.

Moors no longer remain
But their legacy lives on
As relevant today as it was before
And the fig, as sweet as ever.

René, Trevellez, Alpujarras, Spain 2018
With Adrienne

Indonesian Evening

By the shores of Bintan Island
Ran the pathway homeward bound.
Behind them kelong nasty and
Before them trekking most unsound.

For the twilight fell around
Like a cloak of velvet blue
And the fireflies without sound
Masked the danger to the two.

Past the lookout raised on sticks
Well and truly in the forest
Full of imagination's tricks
Clutched the duo each a breast.

Here a waving frond does beckon
There a scrape and rustle rasps
Darker grows behind that's gone
Until a shape before them gasps.

Comes now the famous russet bright?
Sumatra's best and fearsome beast?
Are we to die from tiger fright
None so feared in all the East?

Not really, as a stringy feline
Wide-eyed across the dim lit way,

Flies as pursued by dog divine:
The bipeds, saved from fate, do prey.

Forget the tiger's darkling blight
Avoid the danger of a scare,
Walk your pathways in the light;
Your mind it is which is their lair.

Chris, Bintan, Indonesia 2003

Singapore Working Girl

Last week Hong Kong, Lahore the next,
She shuts the door upon the toad.

Upon a high-stool tooled in wood
A Chinese girl casts off her mind
And sheds her clothes and leans
Aback aslant a cool tiled wall,
And slowly, slowly, slows her time,
Offers it to the window's breeze which
Gently soothes her sightless gaze.

Chris, Clayton West 2005
See Philip Larkin's 'Toads'

Distant Return

Fetishes on the shower floor,
A gorgeous cape thrown on the bed,
An excited voice and so awake:
You, home from Africa.

Talk, excited, talk through jet lag,
'Did you sleep a bit?' No,
But glad and free of burdens
Of the Cape and corporate clowns.

That was last night and now
At my dawn I see you
Quiet among plumped up pillows,
Gentle buffers to your approaching light.

Chris, Ampthill 2005

Flight Fragment

To Sydney one afternoon, the pilot kindly
Banked QF2 over Istanbul to hang
Above coppery glints of minarets and domes.
Over India, the flight darkened and slept,
My book fell from my hands, for me to
Dream of ants at prayer in mosques.

Chris, Ampthill 2008

Medley

Shopping for God

Pilgrims of the 21st century
  no longer flock to redundant shrines
    on distant mountain peaks or, in remote places of wilderness
      where Condors or Tigers roam.

Such idols, as found in stone or ice, as lingams to adore;
  now even more left in the cold.
    Supplanted by many new idols,
      proclaimed as Gods: Hail to the Brands!

The brash colours of Benetton
  vie with the slick tick of Nike
    the sweet smell of Chanel
      and all the world loves a Coke.

In gleaming cathedrals called Malls;
  down reverent aisles they lie upon synthetic altars
    where shoddy sacrifice takes place by those
      possessed by opiates no less powerful than those before.

No longer found in quiet chapels or baroque naves;
  instead, among the braying herd driven by greed,
    demanding to be sated. Maimed by insecurity,
      the masses lean upon their new found crutch and go
        shopping for God.

René, Brighton 2002

Vaginal Vortex

He was still young
with a life yet to come
standing in his field of maize,
yellow from Caribbean sun.

He was not to know
that his life was to end,
so whiplash soon,
from a vaginal vortex at ten.

With intergalactic force
that sucked him into space
through a Hoover-tube of chaos,
he entered nature's womb, apace.

His screams were drowned out
by a roar, not of this earth,
that rent asunder logic
and spread tornados of dearth.

René, Brighton 2004
A man was reported killed in a tornado pipe

Canapés to the Death

Those who strut around
In the canapé land
Of banqueting halls
Plush with blood-red pile
And multicoloured glass
Full with cocktail froth
And exotic ware, upon which
Sits the nouvelle this
And nouvelle that,
Resemble roosters at their feed.

Between the savoury bits
Of mozzarella and chives
Their pecking heads
Pound like pistons
And as they do,
They speak in tongues
Unknown to those
From Peckham Rye
Where urban chic is far removed
From slick routines and easy speak.

Here, in hospitality land
The dream continues
Of urbane chicks
That bubble and squeak
And the only deaths
That cause them

To fall from their perch –
Are from consumption.

> *René, Brighton 2008*
> *Following a Westminster Collection fifth anniversary*
> *reception at Lancaster House, London*

Patriot Game

The thrill of the pursuit is lost to modern sport
(For which now people assemble in the parlour)
Cleansed of game in favour of precious medals bought.

'And what is wrong with winning?' comes a retort,
'Will this not fit and fill our national ardour?
The thrill of the pursuit is lost to modern sport?'

'Go on, you're kidding if you think sport is worth a snort,
When even our Olympians are high on stuff, and more.
Cleansed of game in favour of precious medals bought.'

'Well, is not your chase a guise for the ineffectual sort
Like Newbolt's colonel jammed into Imperial gore,
Whilst athletes bent on breaking bounds, their best time
      sought?'

'No, the chase I mourn is free of drugs and national glory
      fraught,

Free as well of the silliness of statistical lore
And free of the silent cheering of screening millions sought.'

'You are not of us, not very loyal, you should be an export.'
'Patriot, like you I am borne by love, but not of this modern
    whore.'
The thrill of the pursuit is lost to modern sport
Cleansed of game in favour of precious medals bought.

Chris, Hunters Hill 2004
Of the Athens Olympics

Cross

The question that you asked,
Wrought by one on the other,
Of change in me and thee
These ten years since,
Twenty between us lived apart;
Two almost touching tantalising
Parallels sliding by our gaze.

A score of thoughts spring up,
Trying to work it out,
As if the unwindable mainspring
Of shifts and alterations
Is ours to halt

For an instant
Of our thoughtful mood.

But as I try my witness,
And run time's passage
Along which our aging forms
Careen with our silhouettes
Playing upon the cavern wall;
An answer: 'Is reflection our cross to
Bear, penance for inaction?'

Chris, Ampthill 2007

Berlin

In 1951 and seven, I was bussed
To school, Kladow to Gatow in a
Rattling ark of a windowless van past
Bombed-out buildings smelling
Sweetly of old water and oil,
Where once was a rat
At a grey serge corpse;
Past ancients, teeth in bundles,
Shitting in their grounds.
(Mum said they didn't have toilets.)
Women with thick, dark stockings,
Knickers around veiny calves,

Men leaning in long black macks:
All, all lumpen Lowry sticks in sacks.

Chris, Ampthill 2008